HELMSFORD

RAINTREE · MALDON · WITHAM

Page 2

Page 3
Page 33

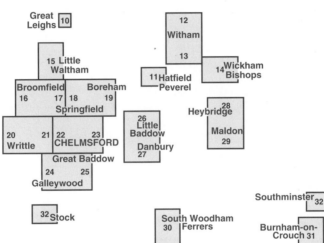

6 Bocki

Rayne 5   Brair
8

Great 4 Dunmow

10
Great Notley

Notley

Great Leighs 10

12 Witham

13

15 Little Waltham

11 Hatfield Peverel

14 Wickham Bishops

Broomfield   Boreham
16   17 18   19
Springfield

26 Little Baddow

28 Heybridge

20   21 22   23
Writtle   CHELMSFORD
Great Baddow

Danbury
27

Maldon
29

24   25
Galleywood

Southminster 32

32 Stock

South Woodham
30 Ferrers

Burnham-on-Crouch 31

Scale of street plans: 4 Inches to 1 Mile (unless otherwise stated)

═══ Motorway	∿ Stream / River
'A' Road / Dual	∿ Canal
'B' Road / Dual	→ One-way Street
Minor Road / Dual	🅿 Car Park
Track	🅲 Public Convenience
Pedestrianized	🄸 Tourist Information
Railway / Station	+ Place of Worship
- - - Footpath	● Post Office

Every effort has been made to verify the accuracy of information in this book but the publishers cannot accept responsibility for expense or loss caused by an error or omission. Information that will be of assistance to the user of the maps will be welcomed.

The representation on these maps of a road, track or path is no evidence of the existence of a right of way.

treet plans prepared and published by ESTATE PUBLICATIONS, Bridewell House, TENTERDEN, KENT. The Publishers acknowledge the co-operation of the local authorities of towns represented in this atlas.

Ordnance Survey® This product includes mapping data licensed from Ordnance Survey® with the permission of the Controller of Her Majesty's Stationery Office.

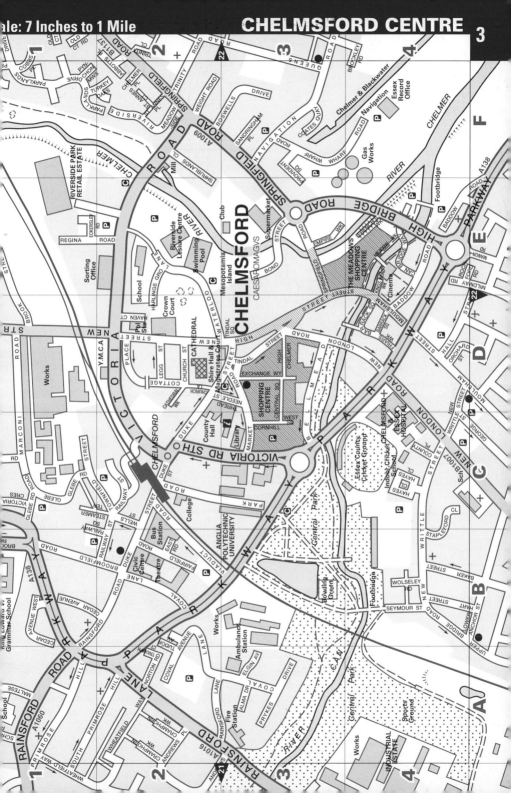

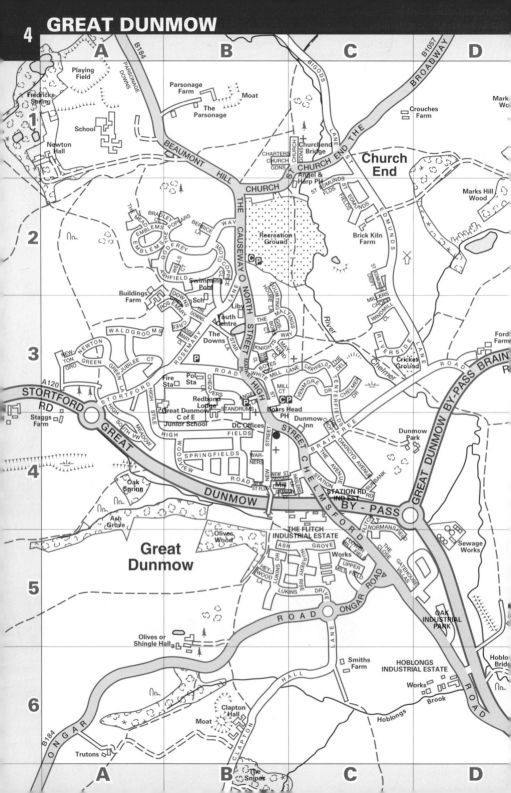

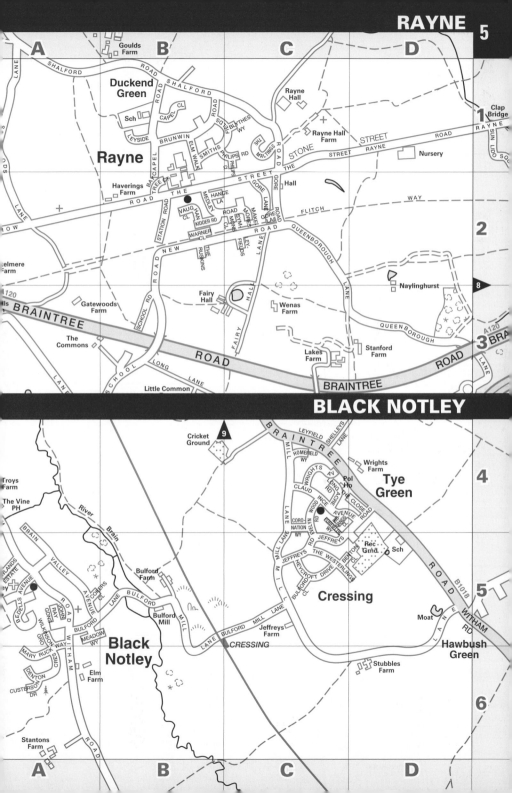

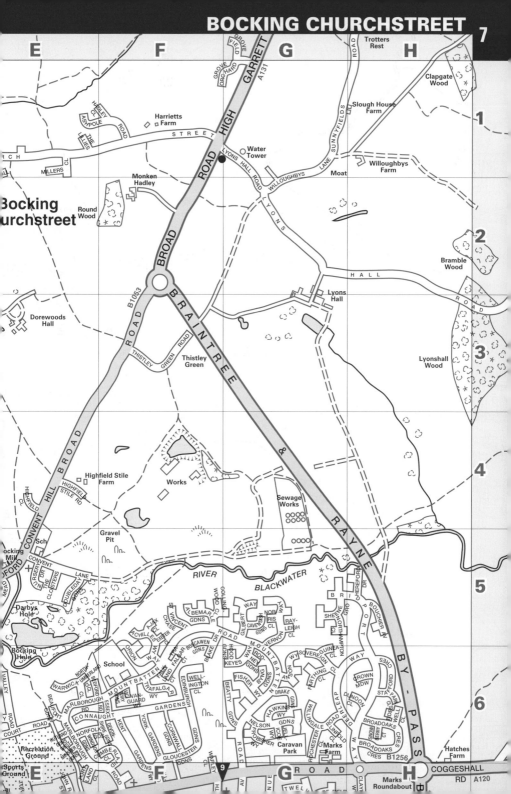

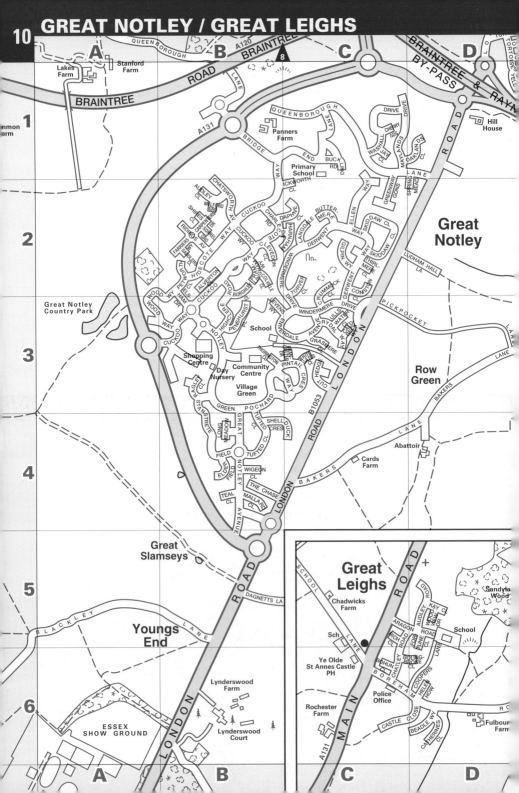

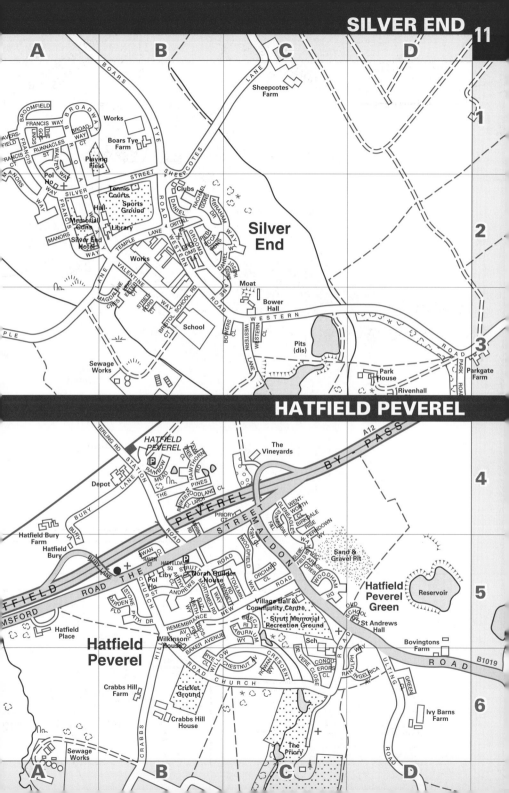

SILVER END

A B C D
1 2 3

Sheepcotes Farm

BOARS LANE

BROOMFIELD
FRANCIS WAY
BROADWAY
BROAD WAY
THE GROVE
Works
Boars Tye Farm
RUNNACLES
WALTER WAY
SILVER
Playing Field
FRANCIS CT
MANORS
Pol Ho
WAY
Tennis Courts
Clubs
Sports Ground
Hall
Memorial Gdns
Library
Silver End Hotel
MANORS
TEMPLE
WAY
VALENTINE
CRES
STREET
Works
STREET
SHEEPCOTES
TYE
STREET
RACHAEL DR
ABRAHAM WAY
DANIEL
GROOMS
CRITTAL LANE
WESTERN RD
DANIEL JOSEPH

Silver End

MAGDALENE CRES
BRISTOL CT
SCHOOL RD
WAY
School
BOWERS RD
Moat
Bower Hall
WESTERN LANE
WESTERN CL
WESTERN
Pits (dis)

Park House
ROAD
PARK ROAD
Rivenhall
Parkgate Farm

Sewage Works

PLE

4 5 6

TERLING RD
HATFIELD PEVEREL STATION
Depot
Hatfield Bury Farm
Hatfield Bury
LANE
BURY
BURY
STATION LANE
RAINBOW MEAD
HAWTHORN RD
THE PINES
LARCH
WOODLAND CL
BIRCH
PEVEREL
STREET
The Vineyards
A12
BY PASS
MALDON
ROAD
PRIORY CT
WENTWORTH
GLENEAGLES
LCL
BIRKDALE RISE
FALDON
WOODFIELD CL
ORCHARD CL
WALNUT
KLEE FIELD
BROADFIELD
CRES
WOODHAM
DR
Sand & Gravel Pit

Hatfield Peverel Green
Reservoir

ROAD
THE
SWAN HAVEN
HATFIELD SQ
Liby
Dorah Builder House
Pol Ho
ST ANDREWS
TOUMIN CL
BENNET
NEW
WAY
Village Hall & Community Centre
Strutt Memorial Recreation Ground
SCHOOL
DE VERE
DR
Sch
St Andrews Hall
Bovingtons Farm
B1019

CMSFORD
ROAD
GARDEN FLD
STONE PATH DR
CHURCH HILL
REMEMBRANCE WAY
Wilkinson House
BAKER AVENUE
MORTIMER RD
ABBEY WAY
WILLOW
CHESTNUT CL
RYE
ROWAN WY
WILLOW
CRESCENT
BIRCH RI
LABURNUM WY
DE VERE RD
CONQUEROR CL
RANULPH WAY
INGELRICA AV
GREEN CL
ULTING
ROAD
Ivy Barns Farm

Hatfield Place
Hatfield Peverel
Crabbs Hill Farm
CHURCH
ROAD
CRABBS
CRABBS
Cricket Ground
Crabbs Hill House
The Priory

Sewage Works

A B C D

Great Totham

Beacon Hill

Wickham Bishops

A   B   C   D

A130   A131

Sheepcotes Wood

Langleys

Chatham Hall

Sheepcotes Cottage

SCURVY HALL LA

CHATHAM

HALL

LANE

SHEEPCOTES   LANE

THE   STREET

Whites Plantation

Sch

Minnow End

The White Hart PH

The Windmill PH

SHEEPCOTES   HILL

Wheelers Farm

WHEELERS   HILL

Little Waltham

CRAPE   DRI

BROOK

CL

WINCKFORD   CL

SCARPELL   CL

BROOK   HILL

CHURCH   HILL

RECTORY   CL

HAZELDON   CL

Balls Farm

The Bell PH

THE   ROAD

LANE

Hall

BACK

WHEELERS   HILL

HILL

ESSEX

Little Waltham Lodge

MANOR   CRES

CHELMER

ROMAN   RD

AVENUE

RIVER   CHELMER

REGIMENT

Sparrowhawk Wood

Merefields

PRATTS   FARM   LANE

Pratt Farm

rts Ground

Rolphs Farm

LANE

BACK

WAY

Montpelier Farm

PRATTS FARM LA

Little Belsteads Farm

LANE

Thorleys Farm

DHOUSE

Sparrowhawk Wood

WOODHOUSE   LANE

LANE

THE MILLARS

COURT   ROAD

Wood House

Croxtons Mill   Weir

BROOMFIELD HOSPITAL

HOSPITAL   APPROACH

THE WINDMILLS

COURT

MANDEVILLE   WAY

WARREN   DRIVE

COMPSTALL

AYLETTS

MAIN   ROAD

B1008

Blasford Hill

Butlers Farm

ESSEX   REGIMENT   WAY

AVENUE

A   B   **17**   C   D

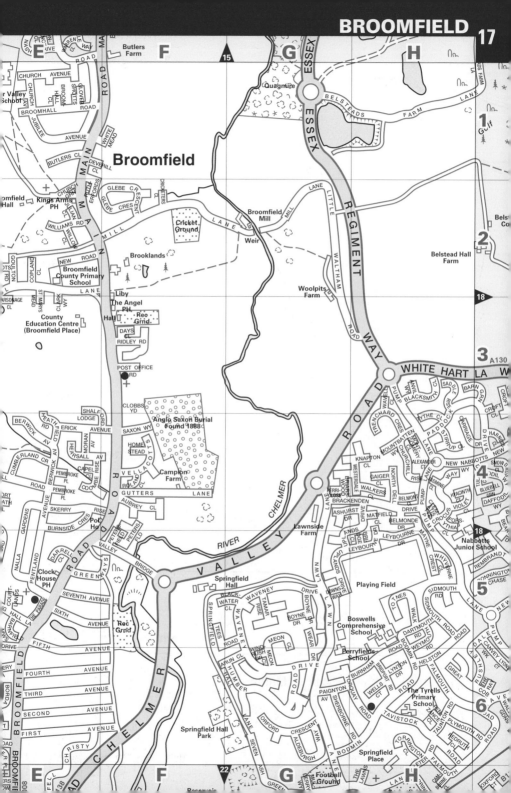

Broomfield

Grid references: E, F, G, H (top and bottom); 1, 2, 3, 4, 5, 6 (right side).

Butlers Farm, Quagmire, Belsteads Farm, Church Avenue, Broomhall, Jubilee Avenue, White Mead, Deverill Cl, Kings Arms PH, Glebe Crescent, Cricketers, Broomfield Mill, Weir, Belstead Hall Farm, Williams Rd, Willow, New Road, Brooklands, Broomfield County Primary School, Woolpits Farm, Liby, The Angel PH, Rec Grnd, County Education Centre (Broomfield Place), Days, Ridley Rd, Post Office, Clobbs Yd, Shalford Lodge, Anglo Saxon Burial Found 1888, Saxon Wy, Home Stead, Campion Farm, Gutters Lane, Aubrey Cl, Lawnside Farm, White Hart La, Blacksmith, Knapton, Mountbatten, Churchill, Alexander, New Nabbotts, Nabbotts Junior School, Springfield Hall, Playing Field, Boswells Comprehensive School, Perryfields School, The Tyrells Primary School, Springfield Hall Park, Springfield Place, Football Ground, River Chelmer Valley, Essex Regiment Way, Broomfield Road.

A130, A15, A18, A22, A808

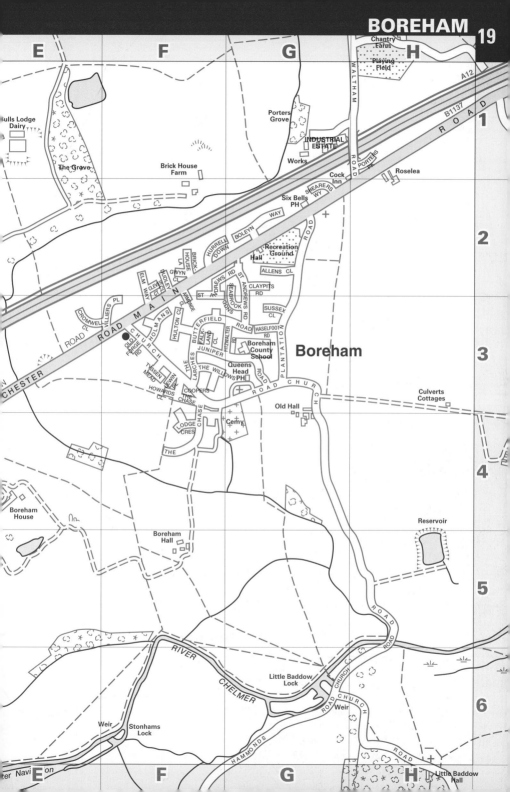

E   F   G   H

1

2

3

4

5

6

Chantry Farm

Playing Field

WALTHAM

A12

B1137 ROAD

Bulls Lodge Dairy

The Grove

Brick House Farm

Porters Grove

INDUSTRIAL ESTATE

Works

PORTERS

ROAD

Cock Inn

Roselea

SHEARERS WY

Six Bells PH

WAY

BOLEYN

HURRELL DOWN

WAY

Recreation Ground

Hall

ROAD

BRICK HOUSE LA

GWYN

ELM WAY

DUDLEY CL

CLEVES

VILLIERS PL

CROMWELL CL

ANDREWS RD

ST ANDREWS RD

ST

ANNINIE

CL

HULTON CL

SEABROOK GDNS

FALKS LAND

FITZWALTER

ROAD

ALLENS CL

CLAYPITS RD

SUSSEX CL

HASELFOOT RD

ROAD

CHESTER

ROAD

ROAD

M A N

CHURCH

HOLMANS

OLD FORGE RD

TISSEN MEAD

LEWIN

THE LARCHES

BUTTERFIELD

JUNIPER

THE WILLOWS

Queens Head PH

Boreham County School

PLANTATION

Boreham

ROAD

CHURCH

Culverts Cottages

HOWARDS CL

THE CHASE

COOPERS

LODGE CRES

THE CHASE

Cemy

Old Hall

Boreham House

Boreham Hall

Reservoir

ROAD

RIVER

CHELMER

Little Baddow Lock

CHURCH

ROAD

Weir

Stonhams Lock

Weir

CHURCH ROAD

HAMMONDS

ROAD

Little Baddow Hall

ter Navi   on

E   F   G   H

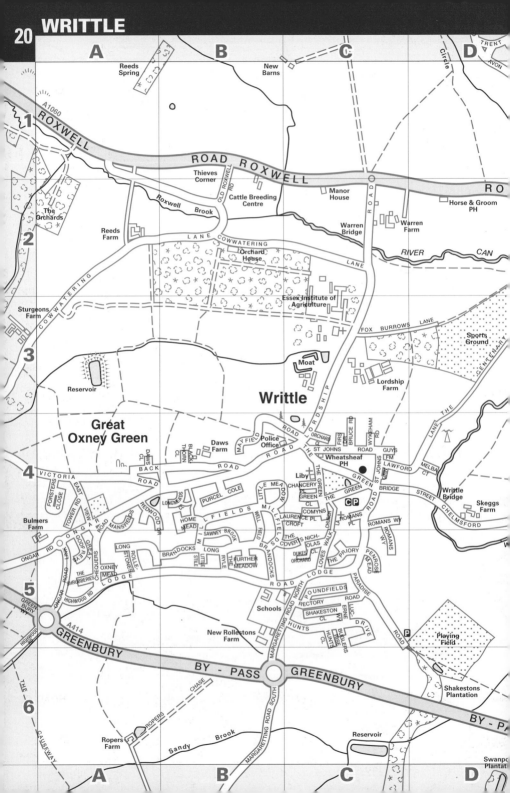

Chelmer Village

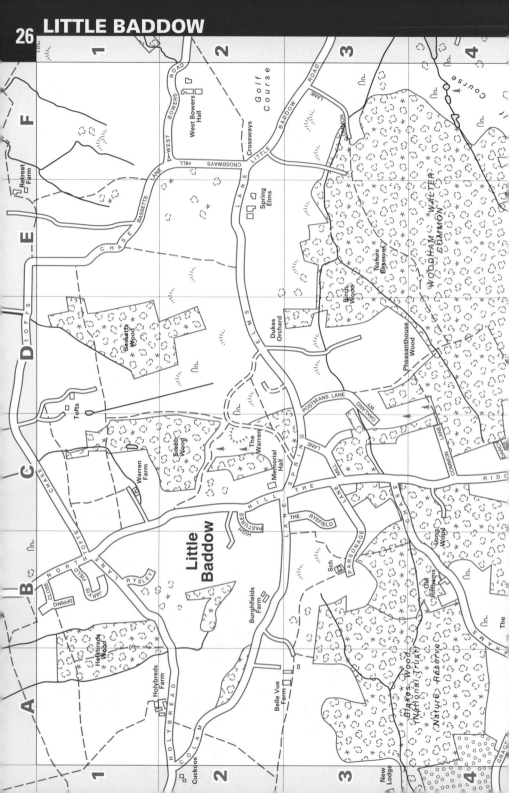

Little Baddow

Heybridge

Langford

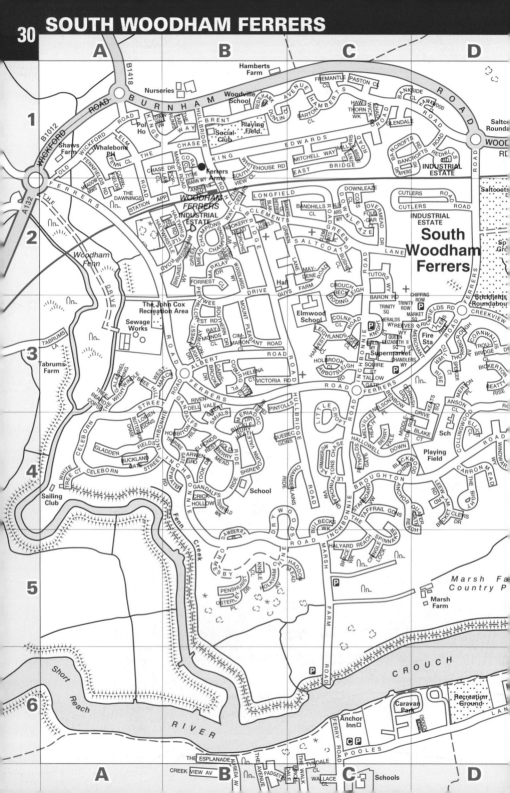

A   B   C   D

Ratsborough Farm

Gravel Pit

Goldsand Bridges

1

Railway Museum

Mangapps

MANGAPP CHASE

MANGAPP CHASE

Cemy.

Stoneyhills

BADGERS KEEP DRIVE

BEAUCHAMPS

COBBINS CHASE

COBBINS GRO.
BOUVEL

Mill Farm

2

Johns Farm

BARNMEAD WAY

CROXON WY

COBBINS WY

ROMAN WY

STONEY HILLS

ROAD

EEN

THE

LANE

SOUTHMINSTER ROAD

ASHWOOD CL

Eves Corner

Pannels Bridge

Romans Farm

Pannels Brook

Brook Farm

ROAD

3

DON

MEADOW WY

ST PETERS FIELD

Hall Farm

CHURCH ROAD

MARSH

GLEBE

GLENDALE

THE LEGS

ROAD

Cherry Garden

COMPASS GDNS

SPRINGFIELD RD

WELLAND ROAD

KING EDWARD AV

St Peters School

MARYS WAY

St Marys C of E Aided Primary School

WORCESTER ROAD

DARCY

RUSSET WY

Burnham-on -Crouch

'Football Ground'

MARYS

PIPPINS

PIPPINS RD

4

URNHAM NESS PARK

EMBER WY

HAMEL WAY

TRENT CL

LIME GRO

ASH GRO

WILLOW WAY

POPLAR

BEECH GRO

CEDAR GRO

BURNHAM

PRINCES RD

EASTERN

ALEXANDRA RD

BLACK WATER CL

HESTER

SAND PIT LN

Sch

SPRINGFIELD RD INDUSTRIAL ESTATE

CHESTNUT CL

ROAD

MILDMAY IND EST

FOUNDRY

SILVERWATER

HERMES CL

FALKLANDS

LANE

DEVONSHIRE RD

ARCADIA

ROAD

WEST CT

LEY

Sch

5

Burnham Riverside Park

DRAGON CL

WAYFARER GDNS

FERNLEA RD

HILLSIDE

PARK

WINSTREE ROAD

GALMADOR RD

Pol Sta

LILIAN RD

ALPHA RD

NEW RD

CROUCH RD

ESSEX RD

MILDMAY RD

NORMANDY AV

ROAD

Sch

Caravan Site

Sports Ground

Mill Field

Warwick Court

Oyster Smack PH

QUEENS RD

WESTERN

ALBERT RD

Clinic
Fire Sta
Amb Sta
Liby

ALAMEIN RD

NELSON RD

ARNHEIM RD

DUNKIRK

WICK RD

RAMBLERS WY

LESLIE PK ROAD

Camp Site

Dengie Hundred Sports Hall

Playing Field

P

REMEMBRANCE AV

CORONATION RD

KINGS CT

REGENTS CT

BRICKWALL

ORCHARD ROAD

PROVIDENCE RD

HIGH ROAD

WITNEY

YORK RD

CHAPEL RD

STEBBINGS

HARBOUR

CALM PATCH

RIVERSIDE RD

SILVER ROAD

ARGYLE

Museum

Marina

White Harte Hotel

Dock

Mus

SHIP RD

STREET

Sch

QUAY

THE BELVEDERE

The Victoria Inn

Camping & Caravan Site

Sewage Works

6

rnham cht our

RIVER CROUCH

Burnham Ferry

Slipways

A   B   C   D

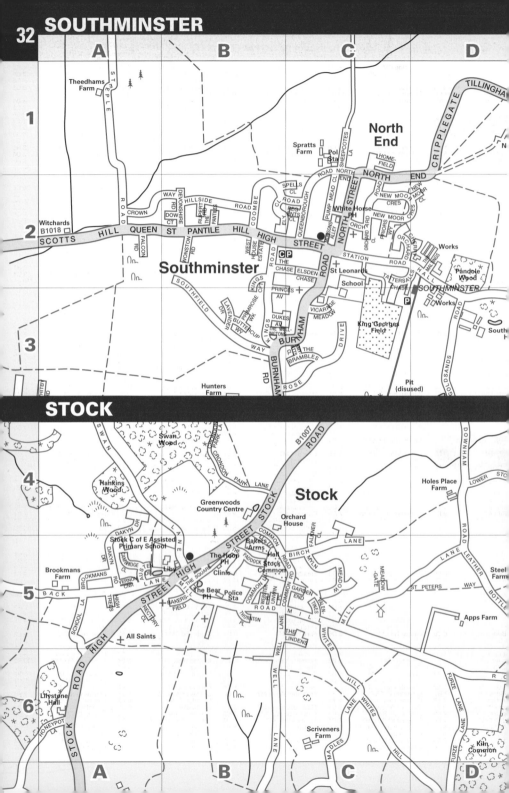

33

Pollys Hill CM7 6 D3
Pork Hall La CM3 10 D6
Portland Cl CM7 9 E1
Progress Ct CM7 8 C1
Pygot Pl CM7 6 C6

Queenborough La,
  Great Notley CM7 10 B1
Queenborough La,
  Rayne CM7 5 C2
Queens Rd CM7 6 D4

Ragley Cl CM7 10 B3
Railway St CM7 9 E1
Rana Ct CM7 6 D6
Rana Dr CM7 6 D6
Rayleigh Cl CM7 7 G5
Rayne Rd CM7 5 D1
Rich Cl CM3 10 C5
Ridings Av CM7 10 B2
Ridlands Cl CM7 9 H6
Rifle Hill CM7 7 E5
River Mead CM7 8 C3
River Vw CM7 7 G6
Rochester Ct CM7 9 G3
Roding Ct CM7 7 G6
Rodney Gdns CM7 7 G6
Roman Ct CM7 9 G3
Romney Cl CM7 6 C4
Rose Gdns CM7 9 E2
Rose Hill CM7 9 E2
Rosemary Av CM7 6 C6
Rue Des Jeunes CM7 8 C2
Russet Cl CM7 9 E3
Rutland Gdns CM7 7 E6
Rydal Way CM7 10 C3

Saddlers Cl CM7 10 B2
St James Rd CM7 6 D5
St Johns Av CM7 8 D2
St Lawrence Ct CM7 8 D1
St Marys Rd CM7 9 E1
St Michaels Ct CM7 8 D2
St Michaels La CM7 8 D2
St Michaels Rd CM7 8 C2
St Peters Cl CM7 8 D1
St Peters in the Fields
  CM7 6 D6
St Peters Rd CM7 6 D6
St Peters Walk CM7 8 D1
St Vincent Chase CM7 7 F5
Salcombe Rd CM7 9 G3
Sandpit La CM7 8 D1
Sandwich Ct CM7 6 C4
Saunders Av CM7 8 B1
Saxon Bank CM7 9 E3
School La CM3 10 C5
School Rd CM7 5 B3
School Walk CM7 8 D1
Scott Cl CM7 9 E4
Sedgefield Way CM7 9 E3
Shakespeare Cl CM7 8 D5
Shalford Rd,
  Panfield CM7 6 A1
Shalford Rd, Rayne CM7 5 A1
Sheene Gro CM7 7 G5
Shelduck Cres CM7 10 B4
Shelley Walk CM7 9 E4
Shelleys La CM7 9 H5
Shires Cl CM7 10 B2
Silks Way CM7 8 D2
Six Bells Ct CM7 6 D5
Skiddaw CM7 10 C2
Skipper Ct CM7 8 C4
Skitts Hill CM7 9 E3
Slough House Cl CM7 9 H3
Smiths Flds CM7 5 B1
Snowberry Ct CM7 7 H6
Sorrel Gro CM7 10 B2
South St CM7 8 D2
Sovereign Cl CM7 7 G6
Spalding Cl CM7 6 C6
Speckled Wood Ct CM7 8 C4
Spencer Sq CM7 6 D2
Springfields CM7 8 A2
Springmead CM7 10 D2
Springmead CM7 8 B1
Springwood Ct CM7 6 A6
Springwood Dr CM7 6 A6
Stafford Cres CM7 7 H6
Stanes Rd CM7 6 C4
Stanstrete Fld CM7 10 B3
Station App CM7 8 D2
Station Rd,
  Braintree CM7 8 D2
Station Rd, Rayne CM7 5 B2
Stephenson Rd CM7 9 E3
Stilemans Wood CM7 9 G4
Stone Cl CM7 8 D2
Stour Ct CM7 9 G4
Strawberry Cl CM7 9 E3
Strudwick Cl CM7 8 C2
Stuarts Way CM7 9 F2
Stubbs La CM7 9 G2
Sun Lido Square Gdns
  CM7 8 A2
Sunnyfields Rd CM7 7 G1
Sunnyside CM7 8 C1
Swan Side CM7 9 E4
Swift Cl CM7 8 B1
Swinbourne Dr CM7 8 B1

Sycamore Gro CM7 8 B2
Symmons Cl CM7 5 C2

Tabor Av CM7 8 C1
Tanners Mdw CM7 9 H2
Teal Cl CM7 10 B4
Telford Rd CM7 8 D3
Templar Rd CM7 9 G2
Tennyson Cl CM7 8 D4
Tenter Cl CM7 6 D5
Thackeray Cl CM7 9 E4
Thames Cl CM7 9 G3
The Avenue CM7 8 D1
The Causeway CM7 6 D6
The Chase, Bocking CM7 6 D3
The Chase,
  Great Notley CM7 10 B4
The Chaseway CM7 9 G2
The Cloisters CM7 7 E5
The Close CM7 9 H6
The Kentings CM7 8 C2
The Ley CM7 9 H3
The Lillies CM7 7 E1
The Lindens CM7 9 E3
The Maltings CM7 5 C1
The Ridgeway CM7 9 E3
The Ruskins CM7 5 B2
The Spinney CM7 9 E2
The Street CM7 5 B2
The Westerlings CM7 9 H6
Thirlmere Cl CM7 10 C2
Thistley Green Rd CM7 7 F3
Thorington Cl CM7 10 B3
Tideswell Cl CM7 7 H6
Tortoiseshell Way CM7 8 C3
Torver Cl CM7 10 C2
Trafalgar Ct CM7 7 F6
Trafalgar Way CM7 7 F6
Trotters Fld CM7 9 F1
Tufted Cl CM7 10 B4
Turnpike Pl CM7 9 E1
Twelve Acres CM7 9 G1

Ullswater Cl CM7 10 C3

Valentines Ct CM7 6 C6
Valley Rd CM7 7 E6
Vanguard Way CM7 7 F6
Vaughan Cl CM7 5 B2
Vauxhall Dr CM7 8 B2
Vernon Way CM7 7 G6
Victoria St CM7 8 D2
Victory Gdns CM7 7 F6

Wall Ct CM7 8 C4
Walnut Gro CM7 8 C2
Warley Cl CM7 7 F6
Warner Cl CM7 5 B2
Warner Dr CM7 6 A6
Warren Rd CM7 9 G2
Warren Side CM7 9 E4
Warshall Dr CM7 10 C1
Warwick Cl CM7 7 E6
Watt Cl CM7 8 D4
Weavers Cl CM7 8 D1
Wellington Cl CM7 7 F6
Wentworth Cres CM7 6 D5
Westergreen Mdw CM7 8 C3
Westminster Gdns CM7 7 E6
Wheatley Av CM7 9 G1
Whitegates Cl CM7 10 C3
Wicks Cl CM7 6 A6
Wigeon Cl CM7 10 B4
Williams Dr CM7 6 D6
Willingale Rd CM7 7 G6
Willoughbys La CM7 7 G2
Windermere Dr CM7 10 C2
Windmill Gdns CM7 7 E1
Windsor Gdns CM7 7 E6
Wingate Cl CM7 6 C6
Winston Cl CM7 6 C4
Wiseman Walk*,
  Sandpit La CM7 8 C1
Witham Rd CM7 8 D5
Wood Way CM7 10 A3
Woodfield Rd CM7 8 D1
Woodlands CM7 9 F1
Woodview Dr CM3 10 D5
Woolpack La CM7 6 D5
Worcester Cl CM7 9 E3
Wordsworth Rd CM7 6 D3
Wrights Av CM7 9 H6

York Gdns CM7 7 F6

BURNHAM-ON-CROUCH

Alamein Rd CM0 31 C5
Albert Rd CM0 31 C5
Alexandra Rd CM0 31 C4
Alpha Rd CM0 31 C5
Arcadia Rd CM0 31 C5
Argyle Rd CM0 31 D6
Arnheim Rd CM0 31 C5
Ash Gro CM0 31 B4

Ashwood Cl CM0 31 B3

Badgers Keep CM0 31 C2
Barnmead Way CM0 31 B2
Beauchamps CM0 31 B2
Beech Cl CM0 31 B4
Belvedere Rd CM0 31 C6
Blackwater CM0 31 C4
Bouvel Dr CM0 31 C2
Brickwall Cl CM0 31 C6

Calmpatch CM0 31 C6
Cedar Gro CM0 31 A3
Chandlers CM0 31 A3
Chapel Rd CM0 31 C6
Chelmer Way CM0 31 A4
Chestnut Cl CM0 31 B4
Church Rd CM0 31 B3
Cobbins Chase CM0 31 B2
Cobbins Cl CM0 31 C2
Cobbins Gro CM0 31 B2
Compass Gdns CM0 31 A3
Coronation Rd CM0 31 B6
Crouch Rd CM0 31 C5
Croxon Way CM0 31 C2

Darcy Cl CM0 31 C4
Debden Way CM0 31 A4
Devonshire Rd CM0 31 A4
Dorset Rd CM0 31 C5
Dragon Cl CM0 31 B5
Dunkirk Rd CM0 31 C6

Eastern Rd CM0 31 C4
Ember Way CM0 31 A4
Essex Rd CM0 31 C5

Fairway Dr CM0 31 B5
Falklands Rd CM0 31 B4
Fernlea Rd CM0 31 B5
Foundry La CM0 31 B4

Galahad Cl CM0 31 B5
Glebe Way CM0 31 C3
Glendale Rd CM0 31 C3
Glynn Rd CM0 31 C4
Granville Ter CM0 31 C6
Green La CM0 31 A2

Hamble Way CM0 31 B4
Hardings Reach CM0 31 C6
Hermes Dr CM0 31 B4
Hester Pl CM0 31 C5
High St CM0 31 C6
Hillside Rd CM0 31 B5
Holly Cl CM0 31 B4
Hornet Way CM0 31 B5

INDUSTRIAL & RETAIL:
Burnham Bsns Pk
  CM0 31 A4
Mildway Ind Est CM0 31 B4
Springfield Ind Est
  CM0 31 A4

King Edward Av CM0 31 B4
Kings Ct CM0 31 B5
Kings Rd CM0 31 B6

Leslie Pk CM0 31 D5
Lilian Rd CM0 31 B6
Lime Way CM0 31 B4

Maldon Rd CM0 31 A3
Mangapp Chase CM0 31 B1
Maple Way CM0 31 A4
Marsh Rd CM0 31 B3
Meadow Way CM0 31 A3
Medway CM0 31 A4
Mildmay Rd CM0 31 C5
Mill Rd CM0 31 B2

Nelson Ct CM0 31 C5
New Rd CM0 31 C5
Normandy Av CM0 31 C6

Orchard Rd CM0 31 C6
Orwell Way CM0 31 A4

Park Rd CM0 31 B5
Pippins Rd CM0 31 C4
Plane Tree Cl CM0 31 B4
Poplar Gro CM0 31 B4
Princes Rd CM0 31 C4
Providence CM0 31 C6

Queens Ct CM0 31 B6
Queens Rd CM0 31 C5

Ramblers Way CM0 31 B6
Regents Ct CM0 31 B6
Remembrance Av CM0 31 B6
Riverside Rd CM0 31 C6
Roman Way CM0 31 C4
Russet Way CM0 31 C4

St Marys Rd CM0 31 B4
St Peters Field CM0 31 A3
Sand Pit La CM0 31 C5
Sheerwater Cl CM0 31 B4

Ship Rd CM0 31 C6
Shore Rd CM0 31 C6
Silver Rd CM0 31 C6
Southminster Rd CM0 31 B2
Springfield Rd CM0 31 A3
Station Rd CM0 31 B4
Stebbing Ct CM0 31 C6
Stoney Hills CM0 31 C2

Thames Way CM0 31 A4
The Belvedere CM0 31 C6
The Cobbins CM0 31 B2
The Leas CM0 31 C3
The Quay CM0 31 A4
Trent Cl CM0 31 A4

Wayfarer Gdns CM0 31 B5
Welland Rd CM0 31 A3
West Ct CM0 31 C5
West Ley CM0 31 C5
Western Rd CM0 31 C5
Wick Rd CM0 31 D6
Willow Cl CM0 31 B4
Winstree Rd CM0 31 B5
Witney Rd CM0 31 B5
Worcester Rd CM0 31 C4

York Rd CM0 31 C6

CHELMSFORD

Abbess Cl CM1 21 E3
Abbotts Pl CM2 3 F2
Abell Way CM2 23 F1
Acres End CM1 21 F1
Admirals Walk CM1 21 F2
Alamein Rd CM1 16 C5
Albany Cl CM1 16 B6
Albra Mead CM2 23 F1
Aldeburgh Way CM1 17 G6
Alder Dr CM2 24 A1
Aldridge Cl CM2 23 E1
Alexander Ct CM1 17 H4
All Saints Cl CM1 22 C1
Allens Cl CM3 19 G2
Alma Dr CM1 3 A3
Alyssum Cl CM1 18 B5
Amcotes Pl CM2 22 A5
Amoss Rd CM2 22 D6
Anchor St CM2 21 H4
Anderson Av CM1 16 C6
Andrews Pl CM1 3 A2
Anjou Grn CM1 18 B4
Anvil Way CM1 17 H3
Apple Way CM2 24 D1
Arbour La CM1 22 B1
Arbutus Cl CM2 24 B1
Archers Way CM2 24 C5
Argyll Rd CM2 18 B6
Armonde Cl CM3 19 F2
Arnhem Rd CM1 16 C6
Arnold Way CM2 24 C4
Arthur Ct CM1 17 F6
Arun Cl CM1 17 F6
Ash Gro CM2 22 B6
Ashford Rd CM1 21 F3
Ashton Pl CM2 23 E3
Ashtree Cl CM1 21 F3
Ashtree Cres CM1 21 F3
Ashurst Dr CM1 17 G4
Aster Ct CM1 18 A5
Atholl Rd CM2 18 B6
Attwoods Cl CM2 24 B5
Aubrey Cl CM1 17 F4
Auckland Cl CM1 16 B6
Avenue Rd CM2 22 B6
Avila Chase CM2 24 B6
Avon Rd CM1 16 A6
Ayletts CM1 15 B6

Back La CM3 15 D3
Back Rd CM1 20 A4
Baddow Hall Av CM2 23 E6
Baddow Hall Cres CM2 23 F6
Baddow Place Av CM2 25 F1
Baddow Rd CM2 3 D4
Badgers Cl CM2 24 B6
Baker St CM2 21 H4
Bakers Mead CM3 15 A2
Bankart La CM2 23 E2
Barclay Cl CM2 25 F1
Bardell Cl CM1 16 C5
Barkis Cl CM1 16 B5
Barlows Reach CM2 23 E1
Barn Grn CM1 17 H3
Barnaby Rudge CM1 16 C4
Barnard Rd CM2 24 C4
Barnes Mill Rd CM2 22 D4
Barnfield Mews CM1 17 E5
Barrack Sq CM1 3 D4
Barrington Cl CM2 25 G1
Beachs Dr CM1 21 E2
Beardsley Dr CM1 18 A4
Beauchamps Cl CM1 18 A3
Beaufort Rd CM2 23 E1
Beaulieu Boulevard
  CM1 18 B4

Beaumont Walk CM1 16
Beeches Cl CM1 21
Beeches Ct CM1 21
Beeches Rd CM1 21
Beehive La CM2 22
Beeleigh Link CM2 22
Begonia Cl CM1 18
Belgrave Cl CM2 22
Bell St CM2 25
Belle Vue CM2 21
Bellmead CM2 3
Bells Chase CM2 25
Belmonde Dr CM1 17
Belmont Cl CM1 17
Belsteads Farm La CM1 17
Belvawney Cl CM1 16
Benidict Dr CM1 21
Berkley Dr CM2 22
Berwick Av CM1 21
Bilton Rd CM1 21
Binley Rd CM2 21
Birches Walk CM2 24
Bishop Hall La CM1 17
Bishop Rd CM1 17
Bishops Court Gdns
  CM2 22
Blacklock CM2 23
Blacksmith Cl CM1 17
Blackwater Cl CM1 21
Bluebell Grn CM1 18
Bodmin Rd CM1 17
Boleyn Way CM3 19
Bond St CM2
Bonnington Chase CM1 11
Borda Cl CM1 1
Boswells Dr CM2
Bouchers Mead CM1 1
Bounderby Gro CM1 16
Bouverie Rd CM2 2
Boyne Dr CM1 17
Brackenden Dr CM1 1
Bradford St CM2 2
Braemar Av CM2 2
Bramston Cl CM2 2
Bramwoods Rd CM2 2
Braziers Cl CM2 2
Brendon Pl CM1 1
Brian Cl CM2 2
Briarswood CM1 1
Brick Kiln Rd CM2 2
Brickhouse La CM3 2
Bridge Cl CM1 1
Bridge St CM1 2
Bridport Rd CM1 1
Bristowe Av CM2 2
Britten Cres CM2 2
Brockley Rd CM2 2
Brograve Cl CM2 2
Brook End Rd CM2 2
Brook Hill CM3 2
Brook La,
  Chelmer Village CM2 2
Brook La,
  Galleywood CM2 2
Brook St CM1 2
Brookhurst Cl CM2 2
Brooklands Walk CM2 2
Broomfield Rd CM1 2
Broomhall Cl CM1 2
Broomhall Rd CM1 2
Brownings Av CM1 2
Bruce Gro CM2 2
Bruce Rd CM1 2
Buckingham Ct CM2 2
Buckleys CM2 2
Bulgers Rise CM1 2
Bullen Walk CM2 2
Bunting Cl CM2 2
Burgess Fld CM2 2
Burghley Way CM2 2
Burnell Gate CM1 2
Burnham Rd CM1 2
Burns Cres CM1 2
Burnside Cres CM1 2
Burton Pl CM2 2
Burwood Ct CM2 2
Butlers Cl CM1 2
Butterfield Rd CM3 2
Byron Rd CM2 2

Camborne Cl CM1 1
Camellia Cl CM1 2
Camelot Cl CM1 2
Campbell Cl CM2 2
Can Bridge Rd CM2 2
Canberra Cl CM1 2
Candytuft Rd CM1 2
Canford Cl CM2 2
Cannon Leys CM2 2
Canterbury Way CM1 2
Canuden Rd CM1 2
Canvey Walk CM1 2
Capel Cl CM1 2
Carnation Cl CM1 2
Carriage Dr CM1 2
Cartwright Walk CM2 2
Cassino Rd CM1 2
Caswell Mews CM2 2
Cathedral Walk CM1 2

Meteor Way CM1 21 G3
Mews Ct CM2 21 H5
Micawber Way CM1 16 B4
Milburn Cres CM1 21 E4
Mildmay Rd CM2 22 A5
Mill La CM1 17 F2
Mill Vue Rd CM2 22 D3
Millbank CM2 23 F2
Millers Cft CM2 25 F1
Millfields CM1 20 B5
Milligans Chase CM2 24 B6
Millson Bank CM2 23 F1
Milton Pl CM1 16 D6
Mimosa Cl CM1 18 B5
Mitton Vale CM2 23 E3
Molrams La CM2 25 H2
Montague Gdns CM1 18 B4
Montgomery Cl CM1 17 H4
Montrose Rd CM2 23 E1
Moran Av CM1 17 E4
Moretons CM2 24 B6
Morris Rd CM2 22 C3
Moss Path CM2 24 C5
Moss Walk CM2 24 B5
Moulsham Chase CM2 22 B5
Moulsham Dr CM2 21 H6
Moulsham St CM2 3 D4
Moulsham Thrift CM2 24 A2
Mountbatten Way CM1 17 H4
Mounthill Av CM2 22 C2
Mulberry Way CM1 22 B1
Multon Lea CM1 18 B4
Murchison Cl CM1 16 C6
Murrell Lock CM2 23 E1

Nabbott Rd CM1 21 E3
Nalla Gdns CM1 17 E5
Napier Ct CM1 16 B6
Nash Dr CM1 15 B6
Navigation Rd CM2 3 F3
Nelson Gro CM1 21 G3
New Bowers Way CM1 18 A5
New Dukes Way CM2 22 D2
New London Rd CM2 3 D4
New Meadgate Ter CM2 22 B5
New Nabbotts Way CM1 17 H4
New Rd, Broomfield CM1 17 E2
New Rd, Great Baddow CM2 25 F1
New St CM1 3 D2
New Writtle St CM2 3 B4
Newcourt Rd CM2 22 C2
Newport Cl CM2 25 G1
Nicholas Cl CM1 20 C5
Nicholas Ct, Chelmsford CM1 21 G4
Nicholas Ct, North Melbourne CM1 16 B5
Nickleby Rd CM1 16 B4
Noakes Av CM2 24 D2
Norfolk Dr CM1 16 D4
North Av CM1 16 D6
North Dell CM1 17 H4
North Dr CM2 22 D6
Northumberland Ct CM2 23 E1
Norton Rd CM1 3 A2
Nursery Rd CM2 21 H5

Oak Lodge Tye CM1 18 B5
Oaklands Cres CM2 21 H5
Oaklea Av CM2 22 C2
Oaks Cotts*, Main Rd CM3 19 F2
Ockelford Av CM1 16 D6
Old Court Rd CM2 22 B2
Old Ct CM2 22 B2
Old Forge Rd CM3 19 F3
Old Roxwell Rd CM1 20 B2
Old School Fld CM1 22 C1
Oldbury Av CM2 22 D6
Oliver Way CM1 16 C4
Ongar Rd CM1 20 A5
Ongar Rd Link CM1 20 A6
Orange Tree Cl CM2 24 C1
Orchard Cl, Tilekiln CM2 24 C2
Orchard Cl, Writtle CM1 20 C4
Orchard St CM2 3 D4
Orford Cres CM1 17 G6
Osea Way CM1 18 A6
Osprey Way CM2 24 A2
Oxford Cl CM2 22 D1
Oxney Mead CM1 20 A5

Paddock Dr CM1 17 H4
Paignton Av CM1 17 G6
Palm Cl CM2 24 C1
Palmers Cft CM2 23 E3
Palmerston Lodge CM2 25 F1
Pan Walk CM1 16 B6
Paradise Rd CM1 20 C5
Park Av CM1 21 G2
Park Rd CM1 3 C3
Park View Cres CM2 25 F2
Parker Rd CM2 22 D2
Parklands Dr CM1 3 F2
Parklands Way CM2 24 C6

Parkway CM2 3 A2
Parsonage Cl CM1 17 E3
Parsons La CM2 24 C5
Partridge Av CM1 16 D6
Paschal Way CM2 22 D5
Patching Hall La CM1 16 D3
Pavitt Mdw CM2 24 C5
Pawle Cl CM1 23 E6
Pearce Manor CM2 21 G5
Peel Rd CM2 22 D1
Peggotty Cl CM1 16 C5
Pembroke Pl CM1 17 E4
Pennine Rd CM1 16 B5
Penrose Mead CM1 20 C5
Pentland Av CM1 17 E5
Penzance Cl CM1 17 H6
Peregrine Dr CM2 24 A3
Perriclose CM1 17 G4
Perrin Pl CM2 21 G5
Perry Hill CM1 3 F1
Pertwee Dr CM2 25 E2
Petersfield CM1 17 F5
Petrebrook CM2 23 E2
Petrel Way CM2 24 C2
Petunia Cres CM1 18 A5
Phoenix Gro CM2 21 G5
Pickwick Av CM1 16 A5
Pines Rd CM1 16 B6
Pipchin Rd CM1 16 C5
Pipers Tye CM2 24 C4
Pitt Chase CM2 25 E2
Plane Tree Cl CM2 24 B2
Plantation Rd CM3 19 G3
Plover Walk CM2 24 A3
Plumtree Av CM2 25 E1
Plymouth Rd CM1 17 H6
Pocklington Cl CM2 23 E2
Pollards Grn CM2 22 D3
Ponds Rd CM2 24 B6
Poplar Cl CM2 24 C1
Poppy Grn CM1 18 B5
Porters Pk CM3 19 H1
Portreath Pl CM1 17 E4
Portway CM2 23 F2
Post Office Rd CM1 17 F3
Pottery La CM1 17 E6
Poundsfield CM1 20 C5
Pratts Farm La CM3 15 D5
Primrose Hill CM1 21 G2
Primula Way CM1 18 B5
Princes Rd CM1 21 G6
Priory Cl CM1 21 F4
Provident Sq CM2 3 E3
Prykes Dr CM1 3 A3
Pryors Rd CM2 24 C5
Pump Hill CM2 25 F1
Pump La CM1 17 H3
Purbeck Ct CM2 24 D2
Purcel Cole CM1 20 B4
Pyms Rd CM2 24 B4
Pynchon Mews CM1 3 F1
Pyne Gate CM2 24 B6

Quale Rd CM2 23 F1
Queen St CM2 21 H4
Queens Rd CM2 3 F3
Queensland Cres CM1 16 B6
Quilp Dr CM1 16 C4
Quinion Cl CM1 16 B4

Railway Sq CM1 3 B2
Railway St CM1 3 B2
Rainsford Av CM1 21 G2
Rainsford La CM1 3 A2
Rainsford Rd CM1 3 A1
Ramshaw Dr CM2 22 D3
Randolph Ter*, Longfield Rd CM2 22 B2
Ransomes Way CM1 22 A1
Raphael Dr CM1 18 A4
Ravensbourne Dr CM1 21 F4
Ray Mead CM3 15 A2
Readers Ct CM2 25 E2
Rectory Cl CM3 15 C3
Rectory La CM1 21 H2
Rectory Rd CM1 20 C5
Redcliffe Rd CM2 21 H5
Redgates Pl CM2 22 C1
Redmayne Dr CM2 21 G6
Redruth Cl CM1 17 H6
Redwood Dr CM1 20 A4
Regal Cl CM2 22 B5
Regency Cl CM1 22 B2
Regina Rd CM1 3 E1
Rembrandt Gro CM1 18 A5
Rennie Pl CM2 22 A1
Renoir Pl CM1 18 A4
Reynards Ct CM2 25 F1
Richardson Pl CM1 21 G2
Richmond Rd CM2 23 E1
Riddiford Dr CM1 21 G2
Ridgewell Av CM1 21 G2
Ridley Rd CM1 17 F3
Riffhams Dr CM2 23 E6
Rignalls La CM2 24 C6
Rivermead CM1 22 A1
Riverside CM2 3 F2
Robert Cl CM2 22 D1
Robin Way CM2 24 A2

Robjohns Rd CM1 21 F6
Rochford Rd CM2 3 E4
Rodney Way CM1 21 F6
Roland Cl CM1 17 F4
Rollestones CM1 20 A5
Roman Rd, Chelmsford CM2 22 A4
Roman Rd, Little Waltham CM3 15 C3
Romans Pl CM1 20 C4
Romans Way CM1 20 C4
Ropers Chase CM1 20 A6
Rose Glen CM2 22 A6
Roseberry Rd CM2 22 A5
Rosemary Cotts*, Brick House La CM3 19 F2
Roslings Cl CM1 16 A5
Rossendale CM1 21 F5
Rothbury Rd CM1 21 E4
Rothesay Av CM2 21 H5
Rothmans Av CM2 25 E1
Roughtons CM2 24 C5
Rous Chase CM2 24 B6
Roxwell Av CM1 21 E2
Roxwell Rd CM1 20 A1
Rubens Gate CM1 18 A4
Running Mare La CM2 24 A4
Rushleydale CM1 18 A6
Ruskin Rd CM1 22 C4
Russell Gdns CM2 24 A3
Russell Way CM1 21 E6
Russets CM2 24 D4
Rutherfords CM1 17 E2
Rutland Rd CM1 17 E5

Sackville Cl CM1 21 F2
Saddle Rise CM1 17 H3
St Andrews Rd CM3 19 G2
St Annes Ct CM2 3 F2
St Annes Pl CM2 3 F2
St Anthonys Dr CM2 24 B1
St Catherines Rd CM1 21 E4
St Fabians Dr CM1 21 F2
St James Pk CM1 21 E1
St Johns Av CM2 22 A5
St Johns Grn CM1 20 C4
St Johns Rd, Chelmsford CM2 21 H5
St Johns Rd, Writtle CM1 20 C4
St Margarets Rd CM2 22 C2
St Marys Cl CM2 25 E1
St Marys Mead CM1 17 E2
St Michaels Rd CM2 22 A5
St Michaels Walk CM2 24 B6
St Mildred Rd CM2 16 H5
St Nazaire Rd CM1 21 F6
St Peters Rd CM1 21 E4
St Vincents Rd CM2 21 H5
Salerno Way CM1 16 C5
Samuel Manor CM2 22 D2
Sandford Mill CM2 22 D3
Sandford Mill Rd CM2 23 E3
Sandford Rd CM2 22 B2
Sandpiper Walk CM2 24 C2
Sandringham Pl CM2 3 F3
Savernake Rd CM1 21 F5
Sawkins Av CM2 24 C1
Sawkins Cl CM2 24 D1
Sawkins Gdns CM2 24 C1
Sawney Brook CM1 20 B5
Saxon Way CM1 17 F4
Saywell Brook CM2 23 E3
School La CM1 16 D3
School La CM1 17 E3
School View Rd CM1 3 A1
Scotts Walk CM1 16 B6
Scurvy Hall La CM3 15 B1
Seabrook Gdns CM3 19 G2
Seabrook Rd CM2 25 F2
Second Av CM1 17 E6
Seven Ash Grn CM1 17 G6
Seventh Av CM1 17 F5
Seymour St CM2 3 B4
Shakeston Cl CM1 20 C5
Shalford Lodge CM1 17 E3
Sharpington Cl CM2 24 C4
Shearers Way CM3 19 G2
Sheepcotes CM2 18 C5
Sheepcotes La CM3 15 C3
Shelley Rd CM2 22 C4
Sheppard Dr CM2 23 E1
Sherborne Rd CM1 17 G6
Sherwood Dr CM1 21 E4
Shire Cl CM1 18 A4
Shropshire Cl CM2 25 F2
Shrublands Cl CM2 3 E2
Sidmouth Rd CM1 17 H5
Silvester Way CM2 23 F2
Sixth Av CM1 17 E5
Skerry Rise CM1 17 E4
Skinners La CM2 24 B4
Skreens Ct CM1 21 E2
Skylark Walk CM2 24 A4
Slades La CM2 24 A4
Smithers Dr CM2 24 A4
Snelling Gro CM2 25 F1
Snowdrop Cl CM1 18 A5
Somerset Pl CM1 17 E4
Sorrell Cl CM3 15 C3

South Primrose Hill CM1 21 G2
Southborough Rd CM2 21 H5
Southend Rd CM2 25 H3
Sowerberry Cl CM1 16 C4
Spalding Av CM1 16 C6
Spalding Way CM2 22 D5
Spenlow Dr CM1 16 A4
Spots Walk CM2 24 C4
Spring Pond Cl CM2 22 C5
Spring Rise CM2 24 B5
Springbok Ho CM2 25 F3
Springfield Grn CM1 22 C1
Springfield Hall La CM1 17 F5
Springfield Park Av CM2 22 B3
Springfield Park Hill CM2 22 B3
Springfield Park La CM2 22 C3
Springfield Park Par CM2 22 C3
Springfield Park Rd CM2 22 B3
Springfield Rd CM2 3 E3
Squirrells Ct CM1 21 F1
Stablecroft CM2 18 A3
Stanley Rise CM2 22 D2
Stanstead Cl CM1 17 H4
Stapleford Cl CM2 3 B4
Steamer Ter CM1 3 C2
Steerforth Cl CM1 16 B4
Stewart Rd CM2 24 A1
Stirrup Cl CM1 17 H4
Stock Rd CM2 24 A4
Stuart Cl CM2 25 G1
Stump La CM1 22 C1
Suffolk Dr CM2 23 E1
Sunflower Cl CM1 18 A5
Sunningdale Rd CM1 21 E1
Sunrise Av CM1 16 D6
Sunrise Av CM1 17 E5
Sussex Cl CM3 19 G3
Sutton Mead CM2 23 F1
Swallow Path CM2 24 A3
Swiss Av CM1 21 G1
Sycamore Way CM2 24 C1
Sydner Cl CM2 25 F2
Sylvan Cl CM2 24 B1

Tabors Av CM2 24 D5
Tamar Rise CM1 17 G5
Tapley Rd CM1 16 C5
Tasman Ct CM1 16 B6
Tattersall Way CM1 21 F6
Taunton Rd CM1 17 H6
Tavistock Rd CM1 17 H6
Taylor Av CM1 16 C6
Tees Rd CM1 17 F5
Tennyson Rd CM1 16 D6
Thames Av CM1 16 A6
The Bringey CM2 25 G1
The Causeway, Great Baddow CM2 25 F1
The Causeway, Writtle CM1 20 A6
The Chase, Boreham CM3 19 F4
The Chase, Great Baddow CM2 25 F1
The Coverts CM1 20 C5
The Dell CM2 25 E1
The Drive CM1 17 E5
The Green, Chelmsford CM1 21 F1
The Green, Writtle CM1 20 C4
The Heythrop CM2 22 C3
The Larches CM3 19 F3
The Lawns CM1 22 C1
The Leys CM2 18 A6
The Limes CM2 24 B5
The Millars CM1 15 B5
The Parade CM1 17 E5
The Priory CM1 20 C5
The Ray CM1 18 A6
The Ridings CM2 24 D1
The Ryle CM1 20 B5
The Shrubberies CM1 20 A5
The Spires CM1 25 F1
The Street, Galleywood CM2 24 B5
The Street, Little Waltham CM3 15 B3
The Westerings CM2 25 F3
The Willows CM3 19 F3
The Windmills CM1 15 B6
Thetford Cl CM1 17 H6
Third Av CM1 17 E6
Thomas Cl CM2 22 D3
Thread Needle St CM1 3 D3
Timsons La CM2 22 D1
Tindal Sq CM1 3 D3
Tindal St CM1 3 D3
Tobruck Rd CM1 16 C5
Torquay Rd CM1 17 G6
Torrington Cl CM1 17 H6
Totnes Walk CM1 17 H5
Tower Av CM1 21 F2
Tower Rd CM1 20 A4
Town Cft CM1 17 E6

Townfield St CM1
Traddles Ct CM1
Trenchard Cres CM1
Trent Rd CM1
Trinity Cl CM2
Trinity Rd CM2
Triumph Ct CM2
Trotwood Cl CM1
Tudor Av CM1
Tugby Pl CM1
Tulip Cl CM1
Tupman Cl CM1
Turkey Oaks CM1
Tusser Ct CM2
Twin Oaks CM2
Twitten La CM2
Tylers Cl CM2
Tyne Way CM1
Tyrells Cl CM2
Tyrells Way CM2
Tyssen Mead CM3
Tythe Cl CM1

Uplands Dr CM1
Upper Bridge Rd CM2
Upper Chase CM2
Upper Moors CM3
Upper Roman Rd CM2

Vale End CM1
Valetta Cl CM1
Valley Bridge CM1
Van Diemans La CM2
Van Diemans Rd CM2
Varden Cl CM1
Vellacotts CM1
Vermeer Ride CM1
Viaduct Rd CM1
Vicarage La CM2
Vicarage Mews CM2
Vicarage Rd CM2
Victoria Cres CM1
Victoria Rd, Chelmsford CM1
Victoria Rd, Writtle CM1
Victoria Rd South CM1
Village Gate CM2
Village Sq CM2
Villiers Pl CM3
Violet Cl CM1

Walford Pl CM2
Walkers Cl CM1
Wallace Cres CM2
Wallasea Gdns CM1
Wallflower Cl CM1
Walters Cl CM2
Waltham Glen CM2
Waltham Rd CM3
Ward Path CM2
Wardle Way CM1
Warren Cl CM1
Warwick Sq CM1
Watchouse Rd CM2
Waterhouse La CM1
Waterhouse St CM1
Waterloo La CM1
Waterson Vale CM2
Wavell Cl CM1
Waveney Dr CM1
Wear Dr CM1
Wedge Copse CM2
Weight Rd CM2
Well Fld CM1
Well La CM2
Well St CM1
Welland Av CM1
Weller Gro CM1
Wellington Cl CM1
Wellmeads CM2
Wells Cl CM1
Wells St CM1
West Av CM1
West Hanningfield Rd CM2
West Lawn CM1
West Sq CM2
Westbourne Gro CM2
Westerdale CM1
Westfield Av CM1
Weymouth Rd CM1
Wharf Rd CM2
Wheatfield Way CM1
Wheelers Hill CM3
White Hart La CM1
Whitebeam Cl CM2
Whitehouse Cres CM2
Whitehead CM1
Whitethorn Gdns CM2
Whitfield Link CM2
Whitmore Cres CM1
Whyverne Cl CM1
Wickfield Ash CM1
Wickham Cres CM1
Wicklow Av CM1
Widford Chase CM2
Widford Cl CM2
Widford Gro CM2
Widford Park Pl CM2

ford Rd CM2 21 F6
kinsons Mead CM2 23 E1
iams Rd CM1 17 E2
oughby Dr CM2 22 D3
ow Bank CM2 24 B5
ow Cl CM1 17 E2
shire Av CM2 22 D2
chelsea Dr CM2 22 C6
ckford Cl CM3 15 C3
drush Dr CM1 17 G6
dsor Way CM1 21 F4
sford Way CM2 18 C5
seley Rd CM2 3 B4
d Dale CM2 25 E1
d St CM2 21 G6
dhall Rd CM1 16 D4
dhill Rd CM2 25 H1
dhouse La CM3 15 A5
dland Rd CM1 21 G1
droffe Cl CM2 23 E2
cester Ct CM2 25 F2
dsworth Ct CM1 16 D6
tle Rd CM1 21 E5
eham Rd CM1 20 C4

vood Rd CM2 22 C3
ham Lock CM2 23 E3
tree Gdns CM2 24 C1
Rd CM2 21 H5

DANBURY / TTLE BADDOW

strong Cl CM3 27 D5

rs La CM3 27 C6
y Mead CM3 27 F7
etts La CM3 26 E1
ers CM3 27 E7
mont Pk CM3 27 B7
edere Cl CM3 27 D6
edere Rd CM3 27 E6
acre Rd CM3 27 B7
La CM3 27 D6

ns La CM3 27 E7
y Garden La CM3 27 E6
tnut Walk CM3 27 D5
s Farm Rd CM3 27 D5
n La CM3 26 A2
nans La CM3 27 B6
mon La CM9 26 F3
mon La CM3 26 C4
Hill CM3 27 C7
sways Hill CM9 26 F2

Ingas CM3 27 B6
ury Vale CM3 27 E7
Rise CM3 26 C4
n CM3 27 F7
vra La CM3 27 E6

Green La CM3 27 A6
Corner CM3 27 C7

ads CM3 27 D6
e La CM3 26 C4
alter La CM3 27 B7

Bowers La CM3 27 D7
owers Rd CM3 27 D7
s La CM3 26 A4
Mdws CM3 27 E7

s Cl CM3 27 E8
rn CM3 27 D6
Pastures CM3 26 B2
eld Cl CM3 27 B7
read La CM3 26 A2
rk Cl CM3 27 D6
ng Jacks La CM3 27 D6
Row CM3 27 B8
rs CM3 27 E7
Grn CM3 27 F7
La CM3 27 F7

Field CM3 26 B1
e Rise CM3 27 E7

sdale CM3 27 E7
ood Cl CM3 27 C6
orough Pk CM3 27 D5
Baddow Rd,
bury CM3 27 D6
Baddow Rd,
e Baddow CM9 26 F2
ields CM3 27 E6
n Rd CM9 27 F6
res La CM3 27 B8

Rd CM3 27 A6
n Rd,
bury CM3,9 27 D7
n Rd,
Bowers CM3,9 27 F8
La CM3 27 C7

Mildmays CM3 27 A6
Mill La, Danbury CM3 27 D7
Mill La,
Little Baddow CM3 26 C3
Millfields CM3 27 E8

North Hill CM3 26 B1
Nursery La CM3 27 D6

Oakland Way CM3 26 C3

Parkdale CM3 27 A6
Parsonage La CM3 26 B3
Pedlars Cl CM3 27 E7
Pedlars Path CM3 27 E8
Penny Royal Rd CM3 27 B7
Plumptre La CM3 27 B8
Postmans La CM3 26 D3
Potters Cl CM3 27 E8
Pump La CM3 27 C8

Riffhams Chase CM3 26 A4
Riffhams La CM3 27 A6
Rumsey Flds CM3 27 D6
Runsell Cl CM3 27 D6
Runsell La CM3 27 D5
Runsell Vw CM3 27 E6
Rysley CM3 26 B1

St Cleres Way CM3 27 B7
Simmonds Way CM3 27 D6
South Hill Cl CM3 27 B7
South View Rd CM3 27 B7
Sporehams La CM3 27 A8
Spring Cl CM3 26 B1
Spring Elms La CM3 26 C3

The Avenue CM3 27 E7
The Common CM3 27 C8
The Hawthorns CM3 27 F7
The Heights CM3 27 A7
The Leeway CM3 27 D6
The Ridge CM3 26 C3
The Ryefield CM3 26 C3
Tofts Chase CM3 26 B1
Twitty Fee CM3 27 E5
Tyndales La CM3 27 F8

Wayside CM3 27 C5
Well La CM3 27 A6
West Belvedere CM3 27 D6
West Bowers Rd CM9 26 F2
Woodhill Rd CM3 27 A7
Woodside CM3 27 D5

GREAT DUNMOW

Angel La CM6 4 B3
Ash Gro CM6 4 B5
Ashfield Cl CM6 4 A2

Beaumont Hill CM6 4 B1
Berbice La CM6 4 B2
Bigods La CM6 4 C1
Boyes Cft CM6 4 B3
Bradley Cl CM6 4 A2
Braintree Rd CM6 4 C4

Charters CM6 4 B1
Chelmer Dr CM6 4 C3
Chelmsford Rd CM6 4 C4
Chequers La CM6 4 B3
Church End CM6 4 C1
Church Gdns CM6 4 C1
Church St CM6 4 B2
Clapton Hall La CM6 4 B6
Coppice Cl CM6 4 B2
Counting House La CM6 4 B2
Crayfields CM6 4 C3

Downs Cres CM6 4 B2

Emblems CM6 4 A2

Flitch La CM6 4 C5

Gatehouse Villas CM6 4 C5
Gibbons Ct CM6 4 B3
Godfrey Way CM6 4 B2
Granary Ct CM6 4 C4
Great Dunmow By-Pass
CM6 4 A4
Green La CM6 4 A3

Haslers La CM6 4 C4
Heywood La CM6 4 B5
High Flds CM6 4 A4
High Mdw CM6 4 A3
High St CM6 4 B3
High Stile CM6 4 A3

INDUSTRIAL & RETAIL:
Hoblongs Ind Est CM6 4 C6
Oak Ind Pk CM6 4 D5
Station Rd Ind Est CM6 4 C4
The Flitch Ind Est CM6 4 C5

Jubilee Ct CM6 4 A3

Knights Ct*,
The Maltings CM6 4 B3
Knights Way CM6 4 B3

Lower Mill Fld CM6 4 C5
Lukins Dr CM6 4 B5

Market Pl CM6 4 B3
Maynard Cl CM6 4 B3
Mill Ct CM6 4 B3
Mill La CM6 4 B3
Millers Cft CM6 4 C3

New St CM6 4 B4
New Street Flds CM6 4 B4
New Street Pas CM6 4 B4
Newton Grn CM6 4 A3
Normansfield CM6 4 C4
North St CM6 4 B2
Nursery Rise CM6 4 C5

Oakroyd Av CM6 4 C4
Ongar Rd CM6 4 A6

Parsonage Downs CM6 4 A1
Randall Cl CM6 4 B3
Riverside CM6 4 C3
Rosemary Cl CM6 4 B3
Rosemary Cres CM6 4 A3
Rosemary La CM6 4 B3

St Edmunds Cft CM6 4 C2
St Edmunds Flds CM6 4 C2
St Edmunds La CM6 4 C1
South Vw CM6 4 A4
Springfields CM6 4 B4
Standrums CM6 4 B3
Star La CM6 4 B3
Station Rd CM6 4 C4
Stortford Rd CM6 4 A3
Sunbank CM6 4 C4

Tenterfields CM6 4 C3
The Avenue CM6 4 C4
The Broadway CM6 4 C1
The Causeway CM6 4 B2
The Close CM6 4 C5
The Croft CM6 4 C4
The Dell CM6 4 C3
The Downs CM6 4 B3
The Maltings CM6 4 B3
The Mead CM6 4 A2
The Poplars CM6 4 B2

Upper Mill Fld CM6 4 C5

Venmore Dr CM6 4 C3

Waldgrooms CM6 4 A3
Warners CM6 4 B4
Wells Ct CM6 4 B2
White St CM6 4 B3
Windmill Cl CM6 4 C3
Woodview Rd CM6 4 B4

HATFIELD PEVEREL

Arthy Cl CM3 11 B5
Ash Cl CM3 11 C4

Baker Av CM3 11 B6
Beech Rise CM3 11 C5
Bennett Way CM3 11 B5
Birkdale Rise CM3 11 C4
Bury La CM3 11 A4

Chelmsford Rd CM3 11 A5
Chestnut Av CM3 11 C6
Church Rd CM3 11 B5
Conquerors Cl CM3 11 C6
Crabbs Hill CM3 11 B6

De Vere Cl CM3 11 C5

Elizabeth Way CM3 11 B5

Ferndown Way CM3 11 C5

Garden Field CM3 11 B5
Glebefield Rd CM3 11 C5
Gleneagles Way CM3 11 C4
Green Cl CM3 11 D6

Hadfelda Sq CM3 11 B5
Hatfield Peverel By-Pass
CM3 11 A5
Haven Ct CM3 11 B5
Hawthorn Rd CM3 11 B4

Ingelrica Av CM3 11 D6

Laburnum Way CM3 11 C5
Larch Walk CM3 11 B4

Maldon Rd CM3 11 C4
Mortimer Rd CM3 11 B5

New Rd CM3 11 C5

Old School Ct CM3 11 D5
Orchard Cl CM3 11 C5

Priory Ct CM3 11 B4
Prospect Cl CM3 11 B5

Rainbow Mead CM3 11 B4
Ranulph Way CM3 11 C6
Remembrance Av CM3 11 B5
Rookery Cl CM3 11 B4
Rowan Way CM3 11 C6
Rye Cl CM3 11 B6

St Andrews Rd CM3 11 B5
Station Rd CM3 11 B4
Stone Path Dr CM3 11 B5
Strutt Cl CM3 11 B5
Sunningdale Fall CM3 11 C4
Swan Cl CM3 11 B5

Terling Rd CM3 11 A4
The Pines CM3 11 B4
The Street CM3 11 B5
Toulmin Rd CM3 11 C5

Ulting Rd CM3 11 D6

Vicarage Cres CM3 11 C5

Wentworth Cl CM3 11 C4
Willow Cres CM3 11 B6
Woodfield Way CM3 11 C5
Woodham Dr CM3 11 C5
Woodland Cl CM3 11 B4

Yew Tree Cl CM3 11 B4

HEYBRIDGE / MALDON

Abbey Turning CM9 28 A3
Abbotsmead CM9 28 C3
Acacia Dr CM9 29 A6
America St CM9 29 C5
Anchor La CM9 28 C3
Anchorage Hill CM9 29 C5
Ash Gro CM9 28 E2
Aveley Way CM9 29 B8
Avocet Way CM9 28 E3

Baker Mews CM9 29 D6
Barnfield Cotts CM9 28 D3
Bates Rd CM9 28 C4
Beacon Hill CM9 29 A5
Beaumont Way CM9 29 D7
Beeches Rd CM9 28 B2
Beeleigh Rd CM9 29 B5
Belvedere Pl CM9 29 B8
Bergen Ct CM9 29 B7
Blythe Way CM9 29 D8
Boulton Cotts CM9 28 D3
Bower Gdns CM9 29 B5
Bridge Ter CM9 28 C3
Broad Street Green Rd
CM9 28 E1
Brompton Gdns CM9 29 B8
Brooke Sq CM9 29 C7
Browning Rd CM9 29 C7
Bull La CM9 29 C5
Burns Cl CM9 29 C7
Butt La CM9 29 C5

Carmelite Way CM9 29 C5
Cedar Chase CM9 28 E3
Centaur Way CM9 29 C8
Chandlers Quay CM9 29 C5
Chaucer Cl CM9 29 C7
Chelmer La CM9 28 C3
Chelmer Ter CM9 29 D5
Chequers La CM9 29 C5
Cherry Garden Rd CM9 29 A5
Chestnut Av CM9 28 E2
Chichester Way CM9 29 D7
Church St CM9 29 D6
Clayton Way CM9 29 D8
Coach La CM9 29 B5
Coates Cl CM9 28 D3
Colchester Rd CM9 28 E3
Coleridge Rd CM9 29 C7
Colne Ho CM9 28 D3
Conyer Cl CM9 29 B8
Coopers Av CM9 28 F3
Courtland Mews CM9 29 C7
Courtland Pl CM9 29 B7
Crayford Cl CM9 29 A8
Creasen Butt Cl CM9 28 C3
Crescent Rd CM9 28 B2
Cromwell Hill CM9 29 C5
Cromwell La CM9 28 B4
Cross Rd CM9 29 C7
Cumberland Av CM9 29 B7

Curlew Cl CM9 28 E3
Cyril Dowsett Ct CM9 29 A5

Darcy Av CM9 29 D7
Dawn Cl CM9 29 D7
De Vere Av CM9 29 D7
Dorset Rd CM9 29 B7
Doubleday Dr CM9 28 B2
Downs Rd CM9 29 C5
Drapers Chase CM9 28 F4
Drayton Cl CM9 29 C7
Dryden Cl CM9 29 C7
Dunlin Cl CM9 28 E2
Dyers Rd CM9 29 C6
Dykes Chase CM9 29 B5

Edward Bright Cl CM9 29 D5
Edwards Walk CM9 29 C5
Eliot Way CM9 29 C7
Elizabeth Way CM9 28 C3
Elm Av CM9 28 E3
Essex Rd CM9 29 B7
Everest Way CM9 28 D2

Fairfield Chase CM9 29 C5
Falcon Flds CM9 29 B8
Falcon Mews CM9 29 B8
Fambridge Cl CM9 29 C7
Fambridge Rd CM9 29 B5
Fir Tree Walk CM9 28 E3
Fitches Cres CM9 29 D6
Francis Mews CM9 29 D7
Freshwater Cres CM9 28 D4
Friars La CM9 29 B5
Friary Flds CM9 29 C5
Fullbridge CM9 28 C4

Galliford Rd CM9 28 C4
Gate St CM9 29 B5
Gate Street Mews CM9 29 B5
Gill Cl CM9 28 B2
Glebe Rd CM9 28 E3
Gloucester Av CM9 29 B7
Goldhanger Rd CM9 28 E3
Granger Av CM9 29 B6
Greenways CM9 29 B6
Guernsey Ct CM9 29 B6

Hadrians Way CM9 28 C3
Hall Bridge Rise CM9 28 E2
Hall Rd CM9 28 D3
Halston Pl CM9 29 B8
Harold Rise CM9 28 C3
Harvest Way CM9 28 B3
Hazelwood Ct CM9 28 E2
Hemmings Ct CM9 29 A7
Heron Way CM9 28 E3
Heybridge App CM9 28 B2
Heybridge St CM9 28 D3
Heywood Ct CM9 28 E2
Heywood Way CM9 28 D2
High St CM9 29 B5
Highlands Dr CM9 29 B5
Hill House Pk CM9 29 C5
Hillary Cl CM9 28 D2
Holloway Rd CM9 28 B2
Hunt Av CM9 28 D3

INDUSTRIAL & RETAIL:
Causeway Ind Est CM9 28 C3
Galliford Rd Ind Est
CM9 28 C4
Heybridge Ho Ind Est
CM9 28 D3
Quayside Pk Ind Est
CM9 28 D4
Riverside Ind Est CM9 28 B4

Jersey Rd CM9 29 D7
Johnston Way CM9 29 C7

Keats Cl CM9 29 C7
Keeble Pk CM9 29 B8
Kestrel Mews CM9 29 D7
King St CM9 29 C6
Kingfisher Cl CM9 28 E3
Kingston Chase CM9 28 B2
Kittiwake Dr CM9 28 E3
Knox Cl CM9 29 C8

Lambourne Gro CM9 29 C7
Langford Rd CM9 28 A1
Lapwing Dr CM9 28 E3
Larch Walk CM9 28 E2
Lawling Av CM9 28 E3
Leslie Newnham Ct
CM9 29 C7
Limbourne Dr CM9 28 F3
Limebrook Way CM9 29 A8
Lindisfarne Ct CM9 29 B7
Linford Mews CM9 29 A8
Lodge Rd CM9 29 B5
London Rd CM9 29 A5
Long Common CM9 28 B3
Longfellow Rd CM9 29 C7
Longfields CM9 29 C5
Longship Way CM9 29 A7

Maldon By-Pass CM9 29 A7
Manse Chase CM9 29 C6

Maple Av CM9	28 E2	
Mariners Way CM9	29 C8	
Market Hill CM9	29 C5	
Markland Ct CM9	29 A7	
Marlowe Ct CM9	29 C7	
Masefield Rd CM9	29 C7	
Mayflower Dr CM9	29 C7	
Mayland Cl CM9	28 F3	
Maypole Rd CM9	28 B1	
Meadway CM9	29 D7	
Meeson Mdws CM9	29 A8	
Memory Cl CM9	29 C8	
Mermaid Way CM9	29 D7	
Midguard Way CM9	29 B7	
Mill La CM9	28 C4	
Mill Rd CM9	29 D6	
Milton Rd CM9	29 C7	
Minster Way CM9	29 B8	
Mirosa Dr CM9	29 D7	
Mirosa Reach CM9	29 C8	
Mount Pleasant CM9	29 B5	
Mundon Rd CM9	29 D6	
Narvik Cl CM9	29 A7	
New St CM9	29 B5	
Newnham Grn CM9	29 B5	
Nightingale Corner CM9	29 C7	
Norfolk Cl CM9	29 A6	
Norfolk Rd CM9	29 A7	
North St CM9	29 D5	
Oak Cl CM9	29 E7	
Oak Rd CM9	28 E2	
Orchard Cl CM9	29 B6	
Orchard Mews CM9	29 B6	
Orchard Rd CM9	29 B6	
Park Dr CM9	29 D6	
Park Rd CM9	29 C6	
Pembroke Av CM9	29 B7	
Plume Av CM9	29 B7	
Poulton Cl CM9	29 D7	
Primrose Walk CM9	29 D7	
Princes Rd CM9	29 C6	
Queen St CM9	29 C6	
Queens Av CM9	29 C6	
Rainbow Mews CM9	28 B3	
Ramsey Cl CM9	28 F3	
Randolph Cl CM9	29 C8	
Redshank Dr CM9	28 E3	
Regency Ct CM9	28 C3	
Ridgeway CM9	29 D8	
Roman Cl CM9	28 C3	
Romanhurst CM9	28 C3	
Rope Walk CM9	29 C6	
Rowan Dr CM9	28 E2	
Royal Ct CM9	29 C6	
Rurik Ct CM9	29 B7	
Rydal Dr CM9	29 D7	
St Giles Cl CM9	29 A6	
St Giles Cres CM9	29 A5	
St Marys La CM9	29 D6	
St Peters Av CM9	29 B6	
Sanderling Gdns CM9	28 E3	
Sandpiper Cl CM9	28 E3	
Sassoon Way CM9	29 C7	
Saxon Way CM9	29 C7	
Scraley Rd CM9	28 E2	
Scylla Cl CM9	28 E1	
Shakespeare Dr CM9	29 C7	
Shelley Cl CM9	29 D7	
Silver St CM9	29 B5	
South House Chase CM9	29 E8	
Southey Rd CM9	28 E3	
Spencer Cl CM9	29 C7	
Spital Rd CM9	29 A6	
Springfield Cotts CM9	28 D2	
Station Rd CM9	28 C4	
Steeple Cl CM9	28 F3	
Stock Chase CM9	28 D3	
Stock Ter CM9	28 D3	
Suffolk Rd CM9	29 A6	
Sunbury Way CM9	29 B8	
Swan Ct CM9	28 D4	
Sycamore Rd CM9	28 E2	
Temple Way CM9	28 B3	
Ten Acre App CM9	28 B2	
Tennyson Rd CM9	29 D7	
Tensing Ho CM9	28 D3	
Tenterfield Rd CM9	29 C5	
The Causeway CM9	28 C4	
The Hythe CM9	29 D5	
The Roothings CM9	28 D3	
The Square CM9	28 D3	
Thirslet Dr CM9	28 E3	
Tideway CM9	29 D7	
Tintagel Way CM9	29 A8	
Towers Rd CM9	28 E3	
Venta Way CM9	29 D7	
Viborg Gdns CM9	29 B7	
Victoria Rd CM9	29 C5	
Viking Rd CM9	29 B7	
Virley Cl CM9	28 F3	
Volwycke Av CM9	29 B7	

Wagtail Dr CM9	28 F3	
Wallace Binder Cl CM9	29 B7	
Wantz Chase CM9	29 C6	
Wantz Haven CM9	29 C6	
Wantz Rd CM9	29 C5	
Warwick Cl CM9	29 C6	
Warwick Cres CM9	29 C6	
Warwick Dr CM9	29 C6	
Washington Cl CM9	29 B6	
Washington Rd CM9	29 A7	
Well Ter CM9	28 E3	
Wellington Rd CM9	29 B5	
Wentworth Mdws CM9	29 B5	
West Chase CM9	29 B5	
West Sq CM9	29 B5	
West Station Yd CM9	29 A7	
White Horse La CM9	29 C5	
Wilsons Ct CM9	29 D5	
Wood La CM9	28 C3	
Wood Rd CM9	28 D2	
Woodfield Cotts CM9	28 E2	
Wordsworth Av CM9	29 C7	

SILVER END

Abraham Dr CM8	11 B2
Boars Tye Rd CM8	11 B1
Bowers Cl CM8	11 C3
Bristol Ct CM8	11 B3
Broadway CM8	11 A1
Broadway Ct CM8	11 A1
Broomfield CM8	11 A1
Crittall Cl CM8	11 B2
Daniel Way CM8	11 B2
Francis Ct CM8	11 A1
Francis Way CM8	11 A1
Grooms La CM8	11 B2
Joseph Gdns CM8	11 C2
Leicester Ct CM8	11 B3
Magdalene Cres CM8	11 A3
Manors Way CM8	11 A2
Manors Way CM8	11 A2
Park Rd CM8	11 D3
Rachael Gdns CM8	11 B2
Rebecca Gdns CM8	11 B2
Runnacles St CM8	11 A1
School Rd CM8	11 B3
Sheepcotes La CM8	11 B1
Silver St CM8	11 A2
Stretford Ct CM8	11 B3
Temple La CM8	11 A3
The Goslings CM8	11 A1
Valentine Way CM8	11 B2
Walter Way CM8	11 A1
Weaversfield CM8	11 A1
Western Cl CM8	11 C3
Western La CM8	11 C3
Western Rd CM8	11 B2

SOUTH WOODHAM FERRERS

Abbotsleigh Rd CM3	30 C3
Akenfield Cl CM3	30 B3
Albert Rd CM3	30 B3
Algars Way CM3	30 C2
Anchor Reach CM3	30 C4
Anson Cl CM3	30 D3
Arwen Gro CM3	30 B4
Ashmans Row CM3	30 C4
Bakers Rd CM3	30 B2
Bancrofts Rd CM3	30 C1
Bandhills Cl CM3	30 C2
Bankside CM3	30 C1
Baron Rd CM3	30 C3
Barton Cl CM3	30 C1
Beatty Rise CM3	30 D3
Becket Way CM3	30 D4
Benbow Ct CM3	30 C3
Berry Vale CM3	30 C4
Bickerton Point CM3	30 D3
Blackwood Chine CM3	30 C4
Blake Ct CM3	30 D4
Brace Walk CM3	30 C5
Brent Av CM3	30 B1
Bressingham Gdns CM3	30 B2
Brickfields Rd CM3	30 D3

Bridgend Cl CM3	30 C1
Broughton Rd CM3	30 C4
Brunel Way CM3	30 B2
Buckland Gate CM3	30 A4
Bucklebury Heath CM3	30 B4
Bulbecks Walk CM3	30 C5
Burnham Rd CM3	30 A1
Bushey Cl CM3	30 C2
Butterbur Chase CM3	30 A4
Bywater Rd CM3	30 B4
Carisbrooke Dr CM3	30 B3
Carron Mead CM3	30 D4
Celeborn St CM3	30 A4
Chadwick Rd CM3	30 B4
Chamberlains Ride CM3	30 C4
Champions Way CM3	30 B2
Chandlers Way CM3	30 C3
Charlotte Cl CM3	30 B3
Chase Dr CM3	30 A1
Chipping Row CM3	30 D3
Cimmaron Cl CM3	30 B3
Clements Green La CM3	30 B2
Clements Pl CM3	30 C3
Clevis Dr CM3	30 D4
Coburg Pl CM3	30 B3
Collingwood Rd CM3	30 D4
Colne Cl CM3	30 C3
Connaught Dr CM3	30 B3
Coral Cl CM3	30 B1
Cornfields CM3	30 A1
Cornish Gro CM3	30 C3
Cornwallis Dr CM3	30 D3
Coxs Cl CM3	30 C2
Creekview Rd CM3	30 D3
Crickhollow CM3	30 B4
Cringle Lock CM3	30 C5
Crouch Beck CM3	30 C2
Crouch Mdws SS5	30 D6
Culver Rise CM3	30 D3
Cutlers Rd CM3	30 C2
Dawberry Pl CM3	30 B5
Downleaze CM3	30 C2
Drapers Rd CM3	30 B3
Drywoods CM3	30 B5
Dunlin Cl CM3	30 B1
East Bridge Rd CM3	30 C1
Edwin Hall Vw CM3	30 A1
Elliot Cl CM3	30 D4
Elm Rd CM3	30 A1
Elronds Rest CM3	30 B4
Fengates CM3	30 B2
Fenn Cl CM3	30 A1
Fennfields Rd CM3	30 A4
Ferrers Rd CM3	30 A2
Ferry Rd SS5	30 C6
Finchland Vw CM3	30 C4
Forrest Cl CM3	30 B2
Foulgar Cl CM3	30 C2
Fremantle Cl CM3	30 B2
Galadriel Spring CM3	30 A3
Gandalfs Ride CM3	30 B3
Gladden Flds CM3	30 A4
Glendale CM3	30 C1
Goldberry Mead CM3	30 B4
Great Smials CM3	30 B4
Green La CM3	30 B2
Green Mead CM3	30 B2
Guild Way CM3	30 C3
Guys Farm Rd CM3	30 B3
Haddon Mead CM3	30 C5
Hallowell Down CM3	30 C4
Haltwhistle Rd CM3	30 A2
Halyard Reach CM3	30 C5
Hamberts Rd CM3	30 C1
Harvest Cl CM3	30 C3
Hawkwood Cl CM3	30 D1
Hawthorn Walk CM3	30 C1
Helena Ct CM3	30 B3
Heralds Way CM3	30 B3
Hillcrest Rd CM3	30 B3
Hither Blakers CM3	30 B2
Hobbiton Hill CM3	30 B4
Holbrook Cl CM3	30 C3
Holkham Av CM3	30 B5
Hullbridge Rd CM3	30 B1
Inchbonnie Rd CM3	30 A4
Keats Sq CM3	30 D3
King Edwards Rd CM3	30 B1
Kings Way CM3	30 A1
Knight St CM3	30 C3
Knole Cl CM3	30 B5
Leeward Cl CM3	30 D4
Leighlands Rd CM3	30 C3
Lettons Chase CM3	30 C4
Littlecroft CM3	30 C4
Long La SS5	30 D6
Longfield Rd CM3	30 B2
Longhams Dr CM3	30 A3
Lorien Gdns CM3	30 A4
Manor Rd CM3	30 B1

Market Sq CM3	30 C3
Marklay Dr CM3	30 B2
Marsh Farm Rd CM3	30 C5
Maydene CM3	30 C2
Meadow Mews CM3	30 C4
Melville Heath CM3	30 A3
Merchant St CM3	30 D3
Meriadoc Dr CM3	30 B4
Merton Pl CM3	30 D3
Middleton Row CM3	30 C4
Millars Cl CM3	30 C1
Mitchell Way CM3	30 C1
Mount Pleasant Rd CM3	30 B3
Nelson Pl CM3	30 C3
Old Wickford Rd CM3	30 A1
Orchid Pl CM3	30 B2
Ormesby Chine CM3	30 B5
Osterley Rd CM3	30 B5
Overmead Dr CM3	30 C2
Paston Cl CM3	30 C1
Penshurst Dr CM3	30 B5
Pertwee Dr CM3	30 B2
Pintolls CM3	30 B3
Pooles La SS5	30 C6
Poplar Cl CM3	30 B1
Quater Gate CM3	30 D4
Quebec Gdns CM3	30 B4
Queen Elizabeth II Sq CM3	30 C3
Raymonds Cl CM3	30 B3
Redhills Rd CM3	30 D1
Redshank Cres CM3	30 B1
Reeves Way CM3	30 C3
Reynolds Gate CM3	30 C4
Rivendell Vale CM3	30 B5
Roding Leigh CM3	30 C3
Rohan Ct CM3	30 B3
Rookery Mead CM3	30 B2
Saltcoats CM3	30 C2
Shirebourn Vale CM3	30 B4
Southern Dr CM3	30 B3
Southview Cl CM3	30 B2
Spencer Ct CM3	30 D3
Squire St CM3	30 C3
Starboard Vw CM3	30 C4
Station App CM3	30 A2
Tabrums La CM3	30 A3
Taffrail Gdns CM3	30 B2
Tallow Gate CM3	30 C3
Tanners Way CM3	30 B2
The Avenue SS5	30 B6
The Bight CM3	30 D4
The Cedars CM3	30 B2
The Chase CM3	30 A1
The Dawnings CM3	30 A2
The Drive CM3	30 A2
The Esplanade SS5	30 B6
The Laurels CM3	30 B2
The Spinnaker CM3	30 C4
The Tabrums CM3	30 B1
The Walk SS5	30 C6
The Withywindle CM3	30 A3
Thorins Gate CM3	30 B4
Thornborough Av CM3	30 D3
Tighfield Walk CM3	30 B3
Took Dr CM3	30 A3
Treebeard Copse CM3	30 A3
Trinity Row CM3	30 C3
Trinity Sq CM3	30 C3
Troubridge Cl CM3	30 D3
Tutors Way CM3	30 C2
Tylers Ride CM3	30 D3
Tythe Barn Way CM3	30 B1
Victoria Rd CM3	30 B3
Westmarch CM3	30 A3
Westway CM3	30 B3
White Tree Ct CM3	30 A4
Whitehouse Rd CM3	30 B1
Wickford Rd CM3	30 A1
Windward Way CM3	30 D4
Woodham Halt*, Hullbridge Rd CM3	30 B1
Woodham Rd CM3	30 D1
Woodlards Way CM3	30 B2

SOUTHMINSTER

Burnham Rd CM0	32 B3
Buttercup Way CM0	32 B3
Cherry Orch CM0	32 C2
Coombe Rd CM0	32 B2
Cripplegate CM0	32 D1
Crown Way CM0	32 A2
Devonshire Rd CM0	32 B2
Dow Ct CM0	32 B2

Dukes Av CM0

Elsden Chase CM0
Ely Cl CM0

Falcon Rd CM0

Goldsands Rd CM0

Hall Rd CM0
High St CM0
Hillside Rd CM0
Homefield CM0

Kings Cft CM0
Kings Rd CM0

Lavender Dr CM0

Munsons Alley CM0

New Moor Cl CM0
New Moor Cres CM0
North End CM0
North St CM0

Orchard Cl CM0
Orchard Rd CM0

Pantile Hill CM0
Primrose Way CM0
Princes Av CM0
Priors Way CM0
Pump Mead Cl CM0

Queen St CM0
Queenborough Rd CM0

Regents Cl CM0
Rose Dr CM0
Rupert Rd CM0

Scotts Hill CM0
Sheepcotes La CM0
Smyatts Cl CM0
Southfield Way CM0
Spells Cl CM0
Steeple Rd CM0

Tattersalls Chase CM0
The Brambles CM0
The Chase CM0
The Maltings CM0
The Pantiles CM0
The Wellingtons CM0
Tillingham Rd CM0

Vicarage Mdw CM0

West House Est CM0
Whitby Rd CM0
Wonston Rd CM0

STOCK

Austen Dr CM4

Back La CM4
Bakersfield CM4
Birch La CM4
Brookmans Rd CM4

Cambridge Cl CM4
Common La CM4
Common Rd CM4
Crondon Park La CM4

Dakyn Cl CM4
Downham Rd CM4

Falkner Cl CM4
Furze La CM4

Garden End CM4

High St CM4
High Trees CM4
Honeypot La CM4

Leather Bottle Hill CM4
Lower Stock Rd CM4

Madles La CM4
Meadowgate CM4
Mill La CM4
Mill Rd CM4
Myln Mdw CM4

Rectory Cl CM4

St Peters Way CM4
School La CM4
Stock Rd CM4
Swan La CM4

The Lindens CM4

For an up-to-date publication list and latest prices visit our web site at

www.estate-publications.co.uk

Use the search facility to find the village, town or city you require.

Local Red Books (selection of)

Ashford & Tenterden
Barnstaple & Ilfracombe
Basildon & Billericay
Basingstoke & Andover
Bath & Bradford-upon-Avon
Bedford
Brentwood
Bromley (London Borough)
Burton-upon-Trent & Swadlincote
Cambridge
Chelmsford, Braintree & Maldon
Chester
Chesterfield
Chichester & Bognor Regis
Colchester & Clacton
Crewe
Eastbourne, Bexhill, Seaford & Newhaven
Exeter & Exmouth
Fareham & Gosport
Folkestone, Dover, Deal & Romney Marsh
Gloucester & Cheltenham
Gravesend & Dartford
Great Yarmouth & Lowestoft
Hereford
Ipswich & Felixstowe
Kidderminster

Kingston-upon-Hull
Lancaster & Morecambe
Lincoln
Macclesfield & Wilmslow
Maidstone
Medway & Gillingham
Newport & Chepstow
Northampton
Norwich
Oxford & Abingdon
Peterborough
Plymouth, Saltash & Torpoint
Reading & Henley-on-Thames
Redditch & Bromsgrove
Rugby
Salisbury, Amesbury & Wilton
Sevenoaks
Southend-on-Sea
Stafford
Swindon
Telford
Tunbridge Wells & Tonbridge
Warwick & Royal Leamington Spa
Weston-super-Mare & Clevedon
Winchester
York

Super Red Books

Birmingham (Colour)
Bournemouth
Brighton
Bristol
Cardiff
Derby
Edinburgh
Glasgow
Leicester
Nottingham
Portsmouth
Southampton (Colour)
Stoke-on-Trent
Swansea

County Red Books

Bedfordshire
Berkshire
Buckinghamshire
Cambridgeshire
Cheshire
Cornwall
Derbyshire
Devon
Dorset
Essex
Gloucestershire
Hampshire
Herefordshire
Kent
Leicestershire & Rutland

Lincolnshire
Norfolk
Northamptonshire
Nottinghamshire
Oxfordshire
Shropshire
Somerset
Staffordshire
Suffolk
Surrey
Sussex (East)
Sussex (West)
Wiltshire
Worcestershire

Estate Publications, Bridewell House, Tenterden, Kent, TN30 6EP
Tel: 01580 764225 Fax: 01580 763720